ENERGY FILES

SOLAR

ENERGY FILES – SOLAR
was produced by

David West ☂ **Children's Books**
7 Princeton Court
55 Felsham Road
London SW15 1AZ

Editor: James Pickering
Picture Research: Carlotta Cooper

First published in Great Britain in 2002 by
Heinemann Library, Halley Court, Jordan Hill,
Oxford OX2 8EJ, a division of Reed Educational
and Professional Publishing Limited.

OXFORD MELBOURNE AUCKLAND
JOHANNESBURG BLANTYRE GABORONE
IBADAN PORTSMOUTH (NH) USA CHICAGO

Copyright © 2002 David West Children's Books

06 05 04 03 02
10 9 8 7 6 5 4 3 2 1

ISBN 0 431 15571 2 (HB)
ISBN 0 431 15578 X (PB)

British Library Cataloguing in Publication Data

Parker, Steve, 1952 -
Solar power. -
(Energy files)
1. Solar energy - Juvenile literature
I. Title
333.7'923

Printed and bound in Italy

PHOTO CREDITS :
Abbreviations: t-top, m-middle, b-bottom, r-right,
l-left, c-centre.

*An explanation of difficult words can be
found in the glossary on page 31.*

ENERGY FILES

SOLAR

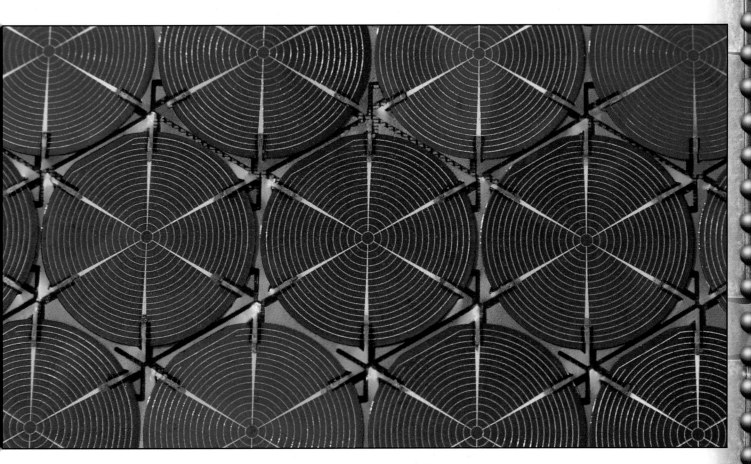

Steve Parker

Heinemann
LIBRARY

CONTENTS

Animals eat other animals, which eat plants, which grow by capturing sunlight. So life is 'solar-powered'.

A go-anywhere radio uses solar power by day, clockwork at night.

INTRODUCTION

When we look around by day, and feel the warmth of summer, we detect solar energy – energy from the Sun. Its light, heat and other rays travel across 150 million kilometres of empty space, to reach us here on Earth. We are using this energy in new ways, to make electricity and drive machines. But the Sun is even more important because other energy sources, like coal, oil, wind and hydroelectricity, were once solar power.

Solar panels change sunlight energy directly into electrical energy. They contain millions of tiny electronic devices known as photovoltaic cells.

Sunlight is strong in space. Big solar panels make enough electricity for a space station.

Solar cells on the face of this wristwatch charge a battery, which stores enough electricity for long, dark times.

The Sun is a star – a giant, burning ball, deep in space. It pours out unimaginable energy of many kinds, which travel or radiate in all directions. Just half of one-millionth of this energy reaches Earth.

Solar energy ranges from radio waves kilometres in length, to gamma rays billionths of a metre long.

SOLAR RAYS

All the types of energy from the Sun are together called solar energy. They are mainly in the form of waves or rays, made of combined electrical and magnetic energy. These waves travel through space at the fastest speed in the Universe, which is the speed of light, 300,000 kilometres per second. In fact, one of the most familiar types of solar energy is light – sunlight. It brightens our world every sunrise, and fades at sunset.

Solar energy is also called electromagnetic radiation – light, heat and other kinds of waves. They make up a range or spectrum of energy with different wavelengths.

Electromagnetic spectrum

Radio waves

Radar waves

Micro-waves

Infrared (heat) waves

Light rays

Ultraviolet waves

X-rays

Gamma rays

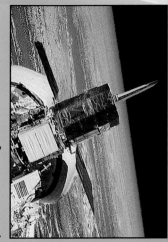

Several satellites, like SolarMax *and* Helios, *have travelled very near to the Sun. They measure its energy and how this is made.*

INSIDE THE SUN

The Sun is an immense fiery sphere 1,400,000 kilometres across. The changes which produce energy happen in its centre or core, at temperatures of 15,000,000°C. Light, heat and other energy types pass through the convection zone, which is like a seething mass of swirling and burning winds, and the radiation zone, which is full of rays, to escape into space from the surface or photosphere.

Plants get energy from sunlight, which they soak up with their leaves and turn into energy-rich foods (see page 24).

Hydrogen core

Convection zone

Radiation zone

Photosphere

SOLAR FUSION

Like all stars, the Sun is made mostly of the Universe's lightest substance, hydrogen. Under tremendous temperature and pressure in the centre, hydrogen 'fuses' or combines with itself to form another substance, helium, plus vast quantities of energy.

Green ISSUES

Solar energy is the most long-lasting or sustainable form of energy we can imagine. But it will not go on for ever. In about 5,000 million years the Sun will run out of the main fuel for its fusion, hydrogen. It will swell into an even bigger but cooler type of star, a red giant, then slowly fade.

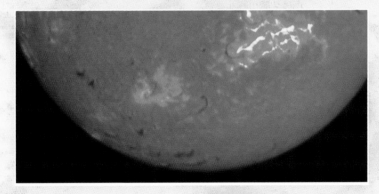

As it swells out, the Sun will swallow Earth.

7

SOLAR-POWERED WORLD

Our energy sources today can be traced back to the Sun, directly or by a series of energy changes.

A hydroelectric dam converts the energy of moving water to electricity.

AIR AND WATER

The Sun warms air and water. Warm air rises, and cool air moves along to take its place. This creates winds, and we can harness their energy by windmills, sailing ships, and wind turbines which generate electricity.

Warm water turns into invisible water vapour, rises into the sky, cools to form droplets in clouds, falls as rain and flows downhill along rivers to the sea. Again, we harness its energy by watermills and hydroelectric power stations.

Hydroelectric power station
Water in the sea is heated to vapour, rises, cools, falls as rain, flows to the sea, and so on, again and again. This is the water cycle.

PREHISTORIC SOLAR ENERGY

Millions of years ago, vast forests grew in sunlit, steamy swamps. Plant remains piled up, were squashed by more layers on top, and slowly turned into coal. In a similar way, billions of tiny living things in the sea died, sank to the bottom, got covered by more layers, and gradually changed into oil and gas. When we burn these three fossil fuels today, we unlock solar energy from long, long ago.

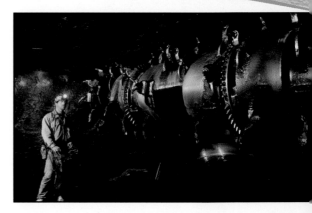

Deep in a mine, coal was once plants that thrived using sunlight as energy.

The Sun pours light and heat on to our world. Various types of power stations change these energy forms, or the effects they have, into our favourite form of energy today – electricity. Electrical energy is convenient, easy to transport, and used by millions of machines, appliances and gadgets, from light bulbs to bullet-trains.

Solar panels change sunlight directly into electricity, with no in-between stage.

Solar power station
This type of power station traps either the Sun's light, by photovoltaic cells, or its heat, by pipes or a solar furnace.

Wind farm
Rows of wind turbines gather the kinetic (movement) energy of air currents, to convert it into electricity in their generators.

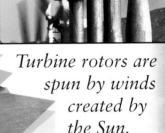

Turbine rotors are spun by winds created by the Sun.

Tidal power
The Sun's pull of gravity causes about one quarter of tidal motion. The Moon's gravity causes the rest.

Fossil fuel power station
Coal, oil and gas are the remains of living things from long ago, which were buried, squeezed and heated in the rocks for millions of years. They became fossils, containing energy in the links or bonds between their various chemical substances. Burning releases the energy as heat and light.

A barrage harnesses tidal energy as sea water flows into a river at high tide, and back out at low tide.

LIGHT TO ELECTRICITY

A solar cell is a small electronic device, usually about the size of a fingernail, that changes sunlight directly into electricity.

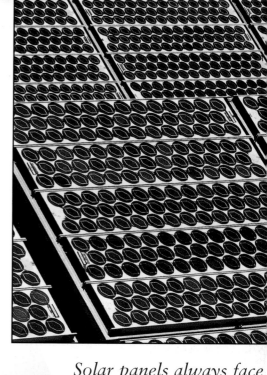

CELLS, PANELS AND ARRAYS

A more correct name for the solar cell is the photovoltaic cell. 'Photo-' is to do with light, while 'volts' measures electricity's strength or pushing force. In bright light a typical solar cell produces only one or two volts, which is about the same as a single torch battery. A solar panel has many solar cells side by side, and a solar array has many solar panels, so the volts add up to give useful amounts of electricity – enough even to power whole cities.

Solar panels always face the direction of the strongest sunlight.

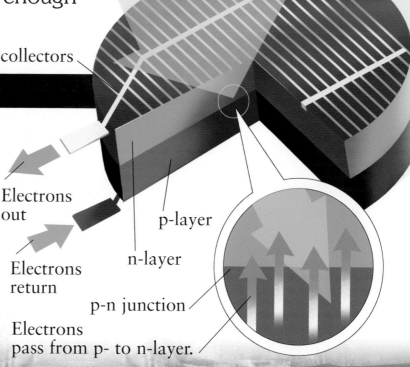

SUNLIGHT

SOLAR CELL

Electron collectors

p-layer

n-layer

p-n junction

Electrons out

Electrons return

Electrons pass from p- to n-layer.

INSIDE A SOLAR CELL

Electricity is a flow of tiny particles called electrons, which are bits of atoms. A single solar cell has two layers of semiconductors (see opposite). One, the n-layer, tends to collect electrons, while the p-layer tries to get rid of them. When light energy hits the surface or junction where the two layers touch, electrons pass from the p-layer to the n-layer, and out around the electric circuit.

Like computer microchips, solar cells are made of semiconductors such as silicon. Certain types also use substances such as gallium, cadmium, boron and arsenic. Some of these materials are rare, and they must be made very pure indeed for use in solar cells. The processes of mining them from Earth's rocks, and purifying them stage by stage, require much energy and produce various waste materials. Some wastes are harmful to the environment and so must be treated to make them safe.

Solar cells require very pure raw materials.

Solar cells

SOLAR PANEL

Rigid backing case

Transparent protective cover

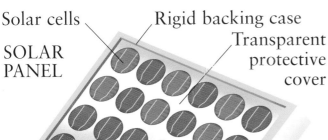

Solar cells are usually small and round, like buttons. This is the best size and shape to collect the electrons, which move or flow to make the electric current.

11

POWER FROM THE SUN

A solar power station is a sunny place where millions of tiny solar cells, arranged on thousands of panels, turn sunlight to electricity.

HOW MUCH POWER?

Each day the total solar energy reaching Earth is far more than the energy we use all around the world. But one-third of it bounces back into space. Much of the rest creates winds and drives the water cycle (see page 8). The amount finally falling on one square metre of ground would, on average, power two or three ordinary light bulbs.

HOW MUCH SUN?

These maps compare solar energy arriving at ground level in different places, over a whole year. The Sun's strength is greatest at the Equator, around the middle of the Earth.

Some regions are often cloudy, so less solar energy reaches the ground. Places such as deserts have fewer clouds – but also fewer people to use the electricity.

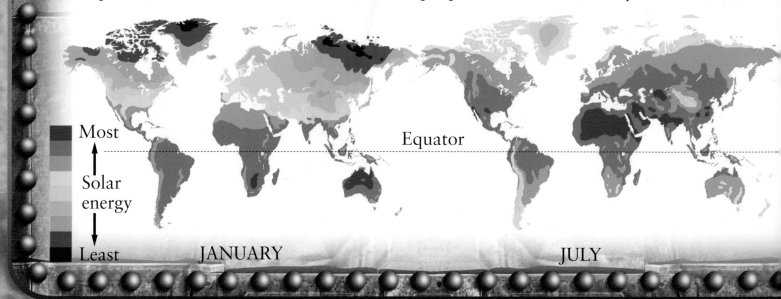

Most

Solar energy

Least   JANUARY

Equator

JULY

Solar panels are cleaned in Europe's largest solar power station in Spain. Controllers (inset) check the amounts of electricity made and fed to the distribution network or grid. Other energy sources 'fill the gap' in the electricity supply at night and on cloudy days.

POWER WHERE NEEDED

Solar power is greatest in places which are sunny and hot all year round. But some of these regions are very far from towns and cities. It would be difficult to carry the large amounts of electricity from a big solar power station to where they are needed.

Green ISSUES

Solar energy is plentiful but weak, spread over a wide area. Even in a very sunny place, to collect enough sunlight to power a town, you would need a solar plant many times larger than the town. This would mean vast areas of solar panels, greatly disturbing nature.

The world's biggest solar plant in the Mojave desert, USA.

SMALLER SOLAR

Solar energy varies through the day and through the seasons. It can be awkward for big power stations to use. But smaller solar panels are springing up like weeds!

PURPOSE-MADE ELECTRICS

Small solar panels are now appearing in many places. Often they provide 'top-up' electricity. If the Sun shines, they can power a light, radio, fridge, telephone or similar device, and charge batteries for cloudy times or during the night.

The Sun provides 'add-on' electricity in many places, such as fast food outlets.

Larger devices such as televisions need more electricity than lights. Batteries and mains electricity provide back-up.

Solar panels are ideal for places where it is tricky to fit electricity cables – such as this flashing float or buoy for ships in Tarifa Harbour, Spain.

Solar panels work better held above low-level dust, as here in central Australia.

This house in Japan can collect enough sunlight for its own electricity needs – with some left over. This can be sold to the local electricity company or utility.

SELF-CONTAINED

Solar cells improve all the time. Older types converted only one-tenth of light energy to electricity. In newer versions, this amount is more than one-fifth. Also, as more solar cells are made, and their designs become more established, the cost per cell falls.

Small solar panels are especially useful in out-of-the-way places where mains electricity (along cables) cannot reach. The panels charge up batteries for 'no sun' periods. Better rechargeable batteries, and improved microchips and other electronic parts which use less electricity, all help 'solar go far'.

Some buildings are now designed 'from the ground up' to use both light and heat from the Sun, and save energy all round, like the University of Northumbria offices, UK.

🌍 *Green* **ISSUES**

As more factories make more solar panels and more solar-powered devices, their costs reduce. An alternative is electricity produced by burning coal, oil or gas, or perhaps bio-fuels. But burning any energy source releases greenhouse gases into the air (see page 27).

Solar lamp factory, India.

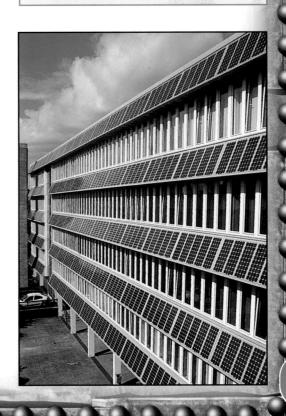

SOLAR 'TO GO'

Almost each month electronic gadgets get smaller, lighter, and less power-hungry. One or a few solar cells can provide enough electricity for them, even in dim light.

CONVENIENT SOLAR

As electronics improve, portable radios and computers, mobile phones, digital cameras and many similar devices shrink in size and weight. The electricity from a few solar cells can power them, and even recharge their batteries (with mains electricity as back-up). This saves energy, raw materials and wastes produced when making disposable batteries.

Calculators and watches were among the first small light-powered gadgets. Solar panels on hats are in an ideal position to power radios and cooling fans.

The Helios *series of light-powered craft include a pilot-less, remote-controlled plane and a super-streamlined car, which give solar much publicity.*

CUTTING EDGE

As part of the advances in electronics, solar cells become smaller, lighter, cheaper and more efficient, too. They find new uses yearly, especially in sunny places with scarce electricity supplies.

Much new information also comes from 'cutting edge' research projects such as solar-powered vehicles, planes and boats. These are not for practical daily use. They aim to provide valuable working experience with solar cells and panels, and also to show the possible and increasing uses of solar power.

Green ISSUES

Inventor Trevor Baylis developed the 'clockwork radio' in the 1990s. Newer versions use both solar energy and a hand-wound clockwork mechanism to charge the batteries. Mains electricity or new batteries are never needed – ideal for remote places, and saving money!

Solar- and self-powered radio, Zambian school, Africa.

High above Earth, in the emptiness of space, there are no clouds or dusty air, no summer or winter. The Sun is undimmed.

WINGS AND DRUMS

A spacecraft needs electricity for its cameras, computer, radio links to Earth and other equipment. There are two main panel designs. Folded 'wings' extend by hinges to their full size after launch, to point at the Sun. 'Drum' panels are for craft that must spin as they travel to keep position and course steady.

ELECTRIC WINGS

Typical satellite panels cover up to 100 square metres and make enough electricity for 50 home light bulbs. Thrusters keep them and the craft facing the Sun.

Solar arrays

Solar panels in array

SUNLIGHT

Computer

Thruster

Batteries

Electricity

Drum-shaped communications satellites like Intelsat VI (inset), being taken into a space shuttle to receive boosters, have solar panels all around. It does not matter which way the satellite faces – some panels are always lit.

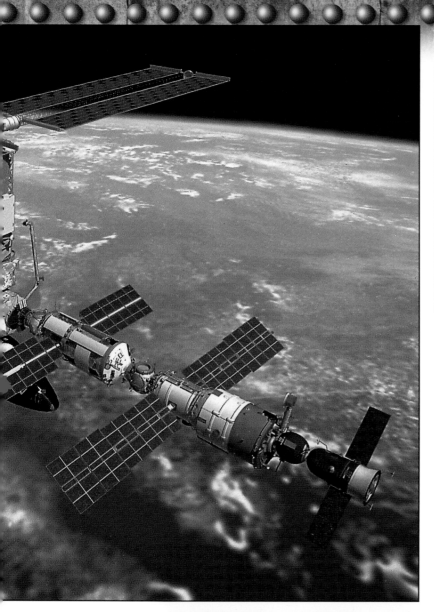

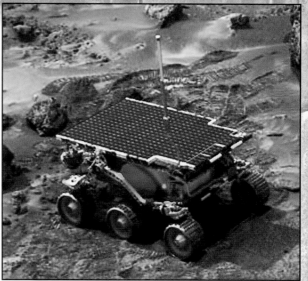

Sojourner *was a skateboard-sized electric vehicle with a solar panel 'roof'. It explored Mars in 1997 and took many amazing photographs, sent back to Earth as radio signals.*

DAY AND NIGHT

Many spacecraft go around, or orbit, the Earth or another world. On the side away from the Sun it is dark and the solar panels cannot work. But the panels charge on-board batteries when lit, for these times of 'night'.

Some deep-space craft go beyond Mars, the next planet away from the Sun after Earth. Here the sunlight is so dim that solar panels cannot work. Such deep-space craft usually carry a small nuclear power plant for electricity.

When complete in a few years, the ISS International Space Station, (above) would just fit on to a soccer pitch. Its panels tilt to face the Sun as the station orbits. The Hubble Space Telescope (right) has run on solar power since 1990.

19

The Sun shines – and burns. Vast amounts of the solar energy we call heat reach Earth. It warms us and our world, and can be put to work.

Heat rays

The Sun's heat passes through space as invisible rays called infrared waves. They are similar in nature to light rays, but each wave is much longer (see page 6). On Earth, infrared waves can be angled and reflected (bounced) by mirrors, just like light rays. In a solar furnace, many mirrors bring all of their heat energy together at one small, very hot place.

SOLAR FURNACE

Many small mirrors tilt to track the Sun and reflect its rays on to a huge curved mirror. This focuses (concentrates) them on to a central tower. Up to 3,000°C of heat can be used to make electricity or for scientific tests.

Curved mirror

Central tower

Reflected rays

Double-reflected rays

Angled mirrors

Since heat and light are the same types of waves, mirrors reflect (bounce) both of them. Curved mirrors focus or concentrate heat into a 'hot-spot'.

The Sun reflects in the main mirror.

In a typical electricity power station, a source of heat boils water into high-pressure steam. This turns a fan-like turbine (below). In many power stations the heat source is burning coal, oil or gas. A solar furnace uses the Sun's infrared rays. These are collected from a huge area by tilting mirrors which bounce them to a central collector on a tower. The rest of the power station is standard.

Solar One *in California, USA has 1,818 mirrors, each 7 by 7 metres. The central tower is 91 metres tall.*

SUN'S RAYS

1 Mirrors track (change angle) as Sun moves across sky.

2 Sun's rays are reflected.

3 Central collector heats sodium.

4 Hot sodium to heat exchanger

5 Water is boiled in heat exchanger.

6 Steam spins turbine and generator.

7 Generator produces electricity.

Excess heat storage tank

Cool sodium back to tower

The collected heat energy is taken up by the substance sodium, which passes it to water in a heat exchanger. The water boils into high-pressure steam which blasts against the angled blades of a turbine, to spin it and the generator on the same shaft.

Shaft

Wire coils and magnets of generator

Steam in

Turbine rotor blades

Used steam

Electricity out

The Sun's heat, like its light, can be used in many ways. Millions of houses, schools, offices and other buildings have solar heating set-ups for warmth and cooking.

TRAPPED HEAT

A greenhouse gets hot because its glass lets through parts of the Sun's energy, and once inside, some of this energy is changed to heat, which the glass traps. Also, a dark object left in the Sun gets hot as it soaks up the Sun's heat, while a bright, shiny object reflects it. These two effects are used to warm water for room heating, washing and cooking, by the solar heating system (below).

Once solar-powered water heaters are fitted, they need almost no attention apart from occasional cleaning, and they last many years.

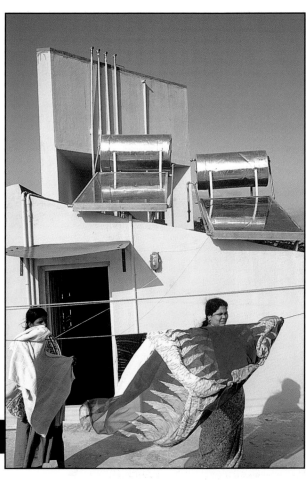

SOLAR HEATING

Water runs through pipes in the solar heating panel, taking in the Sun's heat energy. In the exchanger it passes this to the home hot water supply, for washing or room heating.

Solar water-heating roof panels, England.

SUN'S RAYS

Black heat-absorbing pipes

Heat-retaining glass cover

Hot water to heat exchanger

Heat exchanger

House-hold hot water out

Cold water to panel

House-hold cold water in

Electric pump

The cooker and its stand are carefully turned to keep the mirror facing the Sun. The mirror's specially shaped curve is called a parabola. It reflects almost all the rays into one small area. On a sunny day water can be boiled at 100°C.

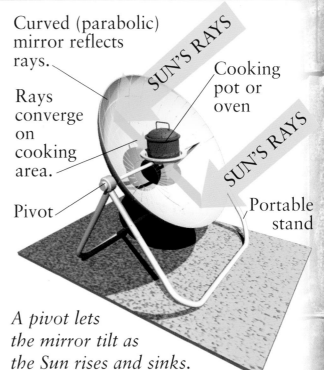

Curved (parabolic) mirror reflects rays.

SUN'S RAYS

Cooking pot or oven

Rays converge on cooking area.

SUN'S RAYS

Pivot

Portable stand

A pivot lets the mirror tilt as the Sun rises and sinks.

COOKING BY MIRRORS

Solar heating systems have no moving parts, apart from a pump to make the water flow slowly. Even simpler is the solar cooker or oven or stove, a home version of the solar furnace power station (see page 21). A curved mirror collects and reflects the Sun's infrared 'heat rays' to a central area, to warm a pan of water or a cooking oven.

Green ISSUES

It may be awkward to store electricity from solar cells. Heat from the Sun can be stored more easily. Hot water is kept in a tank, and food can be cooked while the Sun shines, to eat later. Solar heating has no running costs and is kind to the environment.

Sun-powered meal in India.

Almost all life on Earth relies on solar power. Plants capture the Sun's light energy to live and grow. Animals eat plants, and are eaten by predators, through the food chains of nature.

BUILDING WITH LIGHT

Plants use a process called photosynthesis, 'building with light'. They build or join together carbon dioxide gas from air, water from soil, and energy from sunlight, to make energy-rich substances called sugars.

A big tree has half a million leaves. They can tilt or twist to face the Sun as it moves across the sky through the day.

THE LIVING SOLAR FACTORY

A plant leaf is a living solar factory. It contains a green substance, chlorophyll. This takes in light energy and converts it to chemical energy, in the form of links or bonds between atoms (tiny particles) in the substance glucose sugar.

Photosynthesis needs two raw materials. One is water, which flows up from the roots through tiny tubes inside the plant. The second is carbon dioxide, which makes up a small part of air. It passes into the leaf through tiny holes in its lower surface. A product is oxygen, which living things need to breathe, to stay alive.

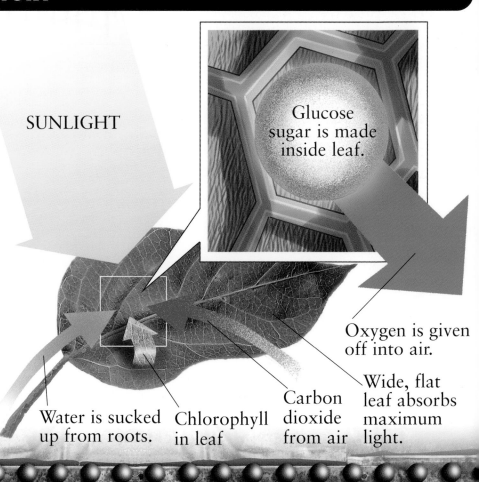

SUNLIGHT

Glucose sugar is made inside leaf.

Oxygen is given off into air.

Wide, flat leaf absorbs maximum light.

Water is sucked up from roots.

Chlorophyll in leaf

Carbon dioxide from air

FEED THE WORLD

The plentiful chemical energy in sugars is released when they are broken apart, back into their simple raw materials. The plant uses the energy to grow and build new parts, and to make seeds with their own energy stores of starches and oils. Scientists are studying photosynthesis to see if we can 'copy' it using machines, as another way to harness solar power.

Solar energy passes to farm crops, and to plant-eaters such as cows, and so to us, in our foods.

ANCIENT SUNLIGHT

Oil (crude petroleum) is made into thousands of products, especially energy-rich fuels such as petrol and diesel. This energy was trapped from the Sun, millions of years ago.

Flames from an oil rig are 'prehistoric sunshine'.

Tiny plant-like living things in the sea (1) carried out photosynthesis, died and sank (2). More layers built up (3). The remains were heated and squeezed deep in rocks to form 'liquid fossil' oil (4, see also page 9).

SUNLIGHT

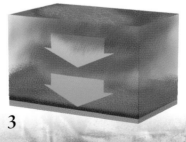

1   2   3   4

SECOND-HAND SOLAR

Plants are a rich store of energy, trapped from the Sun. This energy powers our own bodies, and it can also drive vehicles and machines.

BIOMASS ENERGY

Plants, animals and other life-forms are known as biomass – 'living matter'. Their body substances contain chemical energy, gained second-hand from the Sun. These energy-rich substances can be processed and used as fuels, in many ways.

The Hynol process treats methane, or living or ex-living matter – wood, leaves, animal droppings – with hydrogen gas at great temperature and pressure. It produces the high-energy liquid fuel methanol.

BURNING FUELS

Numerous biomass products, ranging from wood and straw to dried animal dung, are burned as traditional heat sources for warmth and cooking. Rich oils from plants like soya, sunflower, maize, olive, coba and oil-seed rape can fuel specially adapted vehicle engines and power stations.

However, any form of burning produces carbon dioxide and other 'greenhouse gases'. These trap the Sun's heat, and they are causing global warming. Temperatures will rise, climates will change. This will affect nature and farming, and rising sea levels could flood huge areas.

BIOMASS TO BIOGAS

Garden clippings, leftover food, animal droppings, vegetable peelings – put them in the bio-fermenter. The biological (living) processes of rot, decay and fermentation produce methane, the same substance which makes up most of natural gas fuel. The methane collects as a layer and is led away along a pipe, to burn as an energy source for cooking and heating, or in engines.

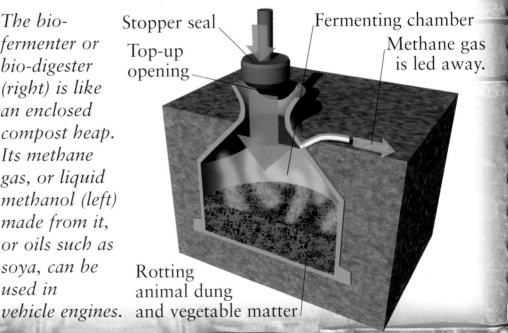

The bio-fermenter or bio-digester (right) is like an enclosed compost heap. Its methane gas, or liquid methanol (left) made from it, or oils such as soya, can be used in vehicle engines.

Stopper seal

Top-up opening

Fermenting chamber

Methane gas is led away.

Rotting animal dung and vegetable matter

27

SOLAR TAKE-OVER?

Solar energy is a vast resource, which is little used at present. Solar cells, panels, arrays, cookers and water-heaters are on the increase. Will solar power ever take over?

LOWER COSTS

Large-scale use of solar power, especially to make electricity, has several drawbacks at present. It does not work all the time, only when the Sun shines, and battery back-up is sometimes difficult. Also, solar cells are still quite costly to make, so their electricity is expensive compared to fossil-fuel power stations burning coal, oil and gas.

New solar cells turn over twice a much light energy into electricity, compared to older versions – and they continue to improve.

A 'solar station' is like a petrol pump for electric vehicles. Banks of solar panels, backed up by huge batteries, charge a car's own batteries when plugged in.

RUNNING DOWN

Fossil fuels are being used up fast, and burning them causes pollution and global warming. Nuclear power, too, creates many hazards. Various forms of solar power, along with hydroelectricity (from running water) and wind power, are sustainable. They cause less pollution and environmental harm. And we can all help, by using less energy all around.

SOLAR CHIMNEY

A solar chimney is a combined greenhouse and wind turbine. A test version has been built in Spain (below left). The Sun heats the ground and air under a vast glass roof.

Hot air rises up the chimney and spins a wind turbine to generate electricity, as more air enters the open sides. Will solar chimney 'farms' (below right) dot deserts in future?

Far above Earth, in space, solar energy is powerful and constant. Could we capture it there and bring it back?

ENERGY BEAMS

Giant solar panels in space could always face the Sun, and convert its light, heat and other forms of energy – probably into electricity. How would we transport this back to Earth? One idea is a type of 'energy beam', perhaps using microwaves. But such ideas are far in the future. For now, most solar energy is earth-bound.

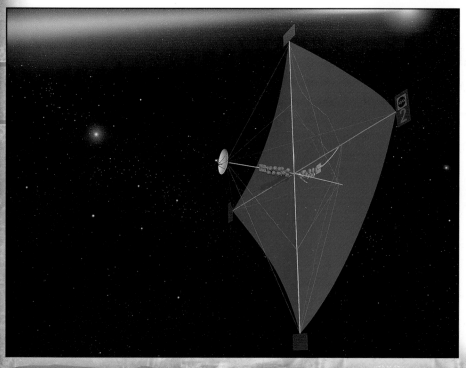

Massive solar panels in space could be built in pieces carried up by space shuttles. And they would last dozens, even hundreds, of years.

The solar space sail unfolds from a small case as a solar panel. Microwave-based energy transfer beams might send the power back to Earth. But their aim would be critical – they could fry or explode the wrong 'target'! And very, very long electricity cables would tangle as the Earth turned far below.

GLOSSARY

electromagnetic
Combined electrical and magnetic forces, such as microwaves, light rays, and heat or infrared waves.

electrons
Tiny objects which are bits of atoms – the basic particles that make up all matter and substance. An electric current is made of moving or flowing electrons.

generator
A machine that turns the energy of movement, usually spinning or rotating, into electricity.

global warming
The rise in temperature all around the world, due to greenhouse gases (see right) in the atmosphere (air). They trap extra amounts of the Sun's heat.

gravity
The force which pulls two objects towards each other, especially the force between large objects such as the Earth, Sun and Moon.

greenhouse gases
Substances in the atmosphere (air) which hold in or retain the Sun's heat. They keep it near to Earth's surface, rather than letting it escape into space, causing global warming (see left).

photosynthesis
The process by which green plants use the energy in sunlight to turn carbon dioxide and water into energy-rich foods, especially sugar.

solar
To do with the Sun.

sustainable
A process or substance that can continue for a very long time, and will not run out, be used up or wear away.

turbine
A shaft (central rod or axle) with a circle of angled blades, like a fan. These spin around when steam or another high-pressure substance blows past them.